Urban Myths

Brandon Robshaw and
Rochelle Scholar

Published in association with
The Basic Skills Agency

Hodder Murray
A MEMBER OF THE HODDER HEADLINE GROUP

Hodder Headline's policy is to use papers that are natural, renewable and recyclable products and made from wood grown in sustainable forests. The logging and manufacturing processes are expected to conform to the environmental regulations of the country of origin.

Orders: please contact Bookpoint Ltd, 130 Milton Park, Abingdon, Oxon OX14 4SB. Telephone: (44) 01235 827720. Fax: (44) 01235 400454. Lines are open from 9.00am to 6.00pm, Monday to Saturday, with a 24-hour message answering service. Visit our website at www.hoddereducation.co.uk

© Brandon Robshaw and Rochelle Scholar 2003, 2006
First published in the Livewire series in 2003 and first published in the Hodder Reading Project series in 2006 by Hodder Murray, an imprint of Hodder Education, a member of the Hodder Headline Group, 338 Euston Road, London NW1 3BH.

Impression number   10 9 8 7 6 5 4 3 2
Year   2011 2010 2009 2008 2007 2006 (twice)

All rights reserved. Apart from any use permitted under UK copyright law, no part of this publication may be reproduced or transmitted in any form or by any means, electronic or mechanical, including photocopying and recording, or held within any information storage and retrieval system, without permission in writing from the publisher or under licence from the Copyright Licensing Agency Limited. Further details of such licences (for reprographic reproduction) may be obtained from the Copyright Licensing Agency Limited, 90 Tottenham Court Road, London W1T 4LP.

Cover photo: Road at night © nagelstock.com/Alamy.
Internal artwork © Gary Andrews.
Typeset by SX Composing DTP, Rayleigh, Essex.
Printed in Great Britain by CPI Bath.

A catalogue record for this title is available from the British Library

ISBN-10: 0 340 91570 6
ISBN-13: 978 0340 915 707

Contents

		Page
1	What is an Urban Myth?	1
2	Buried Alive	3
3	The Exploding Toilet	7
4	Bang Bang	11
5	The Rabbit	14
6	The Hitch-Hiker	18
7	The Kangaroo	21
8	Prawns	24
9	Spider in the Hair	27

1
What is an Urban Myth?

An urban myth is
a modern-day fairy story.
Urban myths are always told as
if they were true.
'This happened to a friend
of a friend,' people say.
Sometimes it happened to a relative,
or someone at work.
Never to the person telling the story.

The people in these stories
never have names.
Dates and places are not given.

Most urban myths are not true at all,
but people believe them.
Then they pass them on.
In this way,
urban myths spread.

Urban myths are found all over the world –
In Europe, America, Africa, Asia and Australasia.
Often the same story
pops up in different countries.

Urban myths are passed on
by word of mouth.
They are not usually written down.
For this reason,
there can be different versions
of the same story.

Some urban myths are very old.
They have been told for hundreds of years
and are still popular.
Some urban myths are funny.
Others are scary.
They are all entertaining.

2
Buried Alive

This is a popular urban myth.
It has been around a long time.
There are a number of different versions.

A friend's great-grandmother dies.
The husband is very upset.
They have lived together for fifty years.
He cannot believe she is dead.
At the funeral,
he does not want her to be buried.
'She's still alive!' he says.
'She's just sleeping!
You can't bury her!'

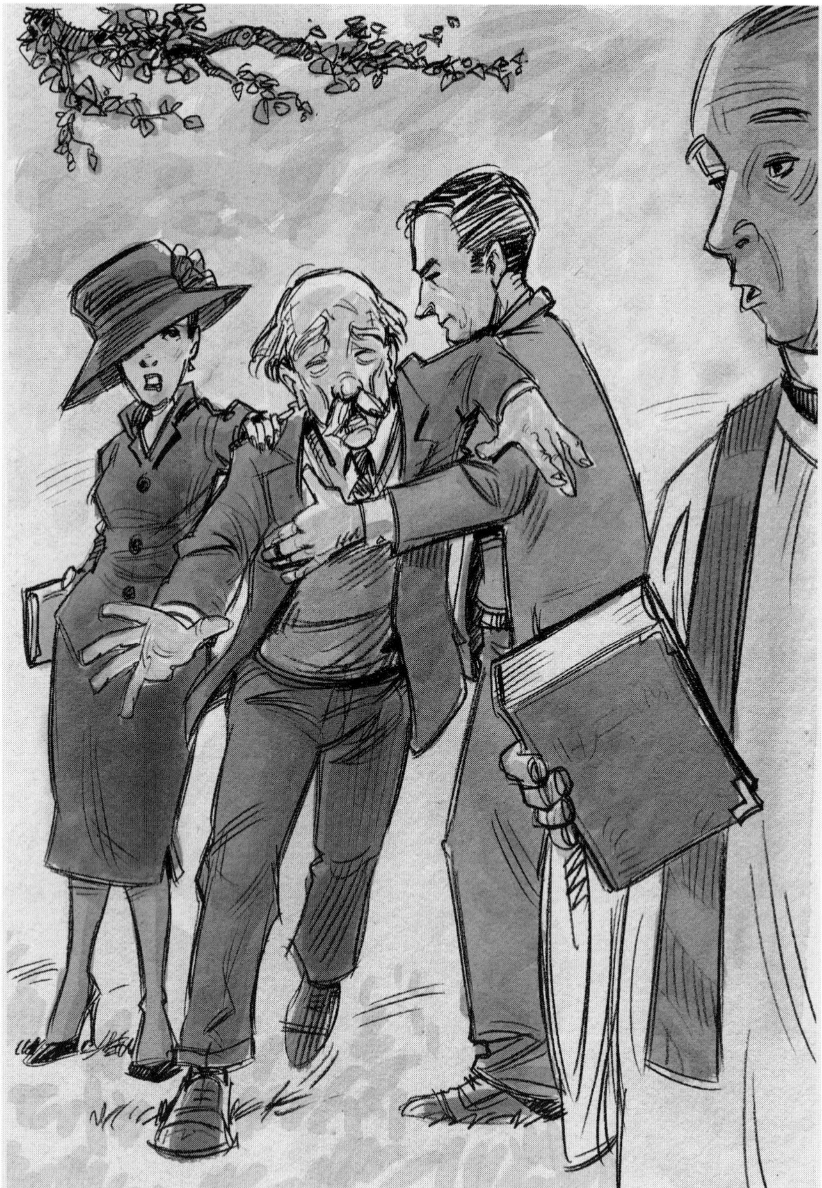

His son and daughter calm him down.
The doctor is there.
He tells the old man
that his wife really is dead.
'She's at peace now,' he says.
'Let her body be buried.'
The old man watches as the coffin
is lowered into the ground.

The old man goes home
but he keeps having bad dreams.
Night after night,
he dreams his wife is alive,
buried underground,
shouting and screaming,
trying to get out of the coffin.

After a week of this,
he goes back to the doctor.
'Please!' he says.
'I know she's still alive!
You must dig her up!'

In the end, the doctor agrees
because he thinks that
if the old man sees his wife
is really dead,
he might begin to accept it.

He arranges for the body to be dug up.
The old man is there
as the doctor raises the coffin lid.

The old woman is dead, sure enough.
But her mouth is wide open
and her fingernails are broken.
There are scratches
on the inside of the coffin lid.

3
The Exploding Toilet

If you're ever having a bad day,
be glad this didn't happen to you.

One Saturday,
a man was mowing his lawn.
The mower ran out of petrol.
He went through the house
to get a can of petrol from the garage.
He filled the mower up.
He finished mowing the lawn.
Then he took the petrol back
through the house – or tried to.

His wife had closed the French windows!
He walked straight into them
and cut himself quite badly.
He also dropped the can of petrol.

He was rushed to hospital.
His wounds were stitched up.
While he was in hospital,
his wife cleared up.
She mopped up the spilled petrol
with kitchen roll.
She threw it down the toilet.

The man came home,
all stitched up and smoking a cigarette.
He went to the toilet.
He sat down.
He threw his cigarette
in the toilet.

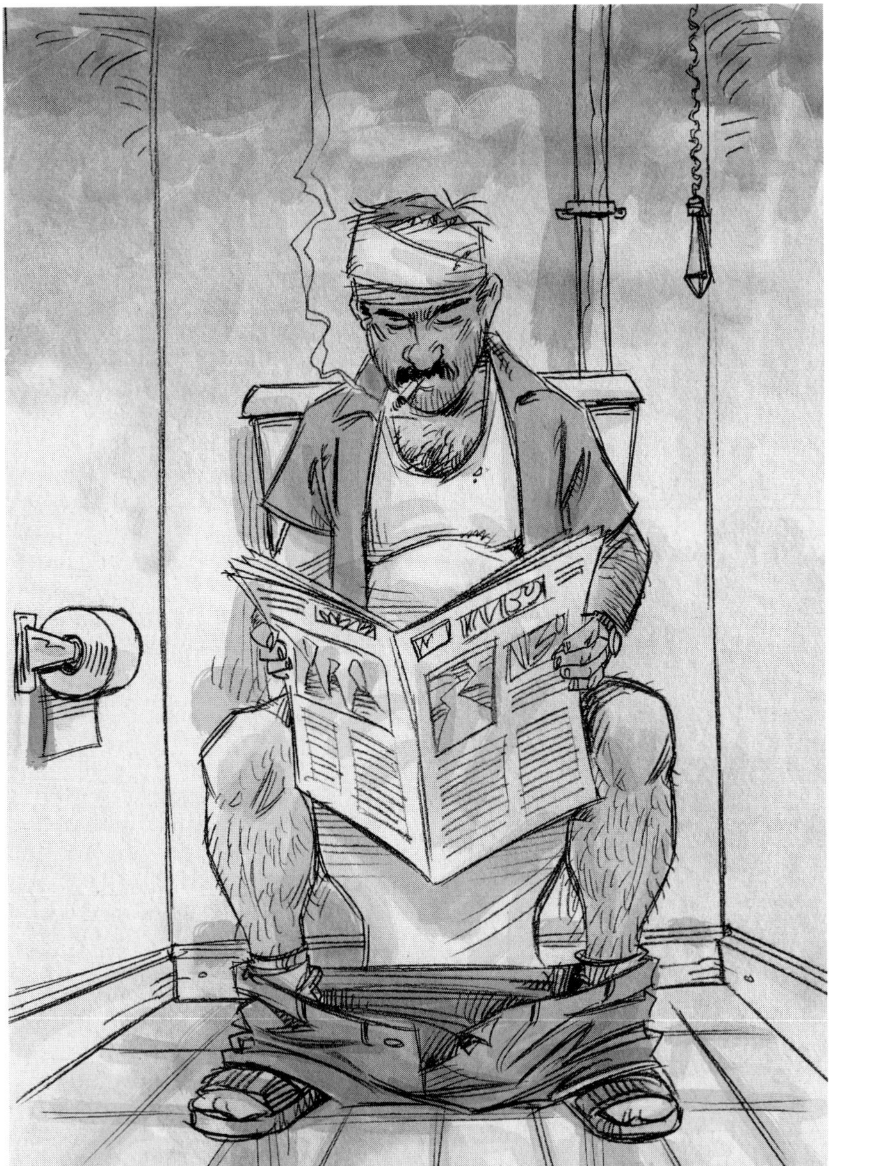

Whoosh!
The cigarette set light to the petrol.
The toilet exploded.
The man was blown across the room.
His buttocks were badly burned.

For the second time that day,
his wife called the ambulance.
The ambulance workers
carried him downstairs.
They asked him what had happened.

When he told them,
they laughed so much
they dropped the stretcher.
The man fell down the stairs
and broke both his legs.

4
Bang Bang

Some urban myths are horror stories.

A young woman and her boyfriend
are on holiday.
They are driving through the countryside.
It is night-time.
They are a bit worried because
they have heard that a dangerous maniac
has escaped from a mental hospital.

Then they run out of petrol.
The boy says that he'll go and get some.
He tells his girlfriend to stay in the car
and keep the doors locked.
Then he walks away into the night.

Time goes by.
The boy doesn't come back.
The girl gets more and more worried.
Her boyfriend's been gone nearly an hour.
What should she do?
Should she get out of the car
and look for him?

Then she hears a loud banging noise
on the roof of the car.

Bang! Bang! Bang!
She is terrified.
With relief, she sees a group of policemen
running towards the car.
One of them comes up to the window.

'Don't worry, madam,' he says.
'The car is surrounded.
You are quite safe.
Get out of the car now.
Walk away and do NOT look back!'

The girl gets out of the car.
She walks a little way.
The banging noise is still going on.
She can't help looking back.

The maniac is sitting on top of the car.
He has her boyfriend's head in his hands.
Just the head.
He is banging it on the roof.

5
The Rabbit

A young couple owned a dog.
A Doberman.
It looked very fierce,
but was really quite a gentle animal.

One day the couple's neighbours
went away for the weekend.
The next morning,
the couple saw their dog.

It was running round the garden
with something in its mouth.
It was next-door's rabbit!
Somehow, the dog must have pulled
the rabbit from its hutch.

They ran out into the garden,
smacked their dog,
and made it drop the rabbit.
It was too late.
The rabbit was dead.

What could they do?
They didn't want to tell their neighbours.
Their neighbours would be angry.
They might even say
the dog should be put down.

The couple took the rabbit
into the kitchen and cleaned it up.
They washed all the mud off.
They found that there was no blood.
The rabbit must have died of shock.

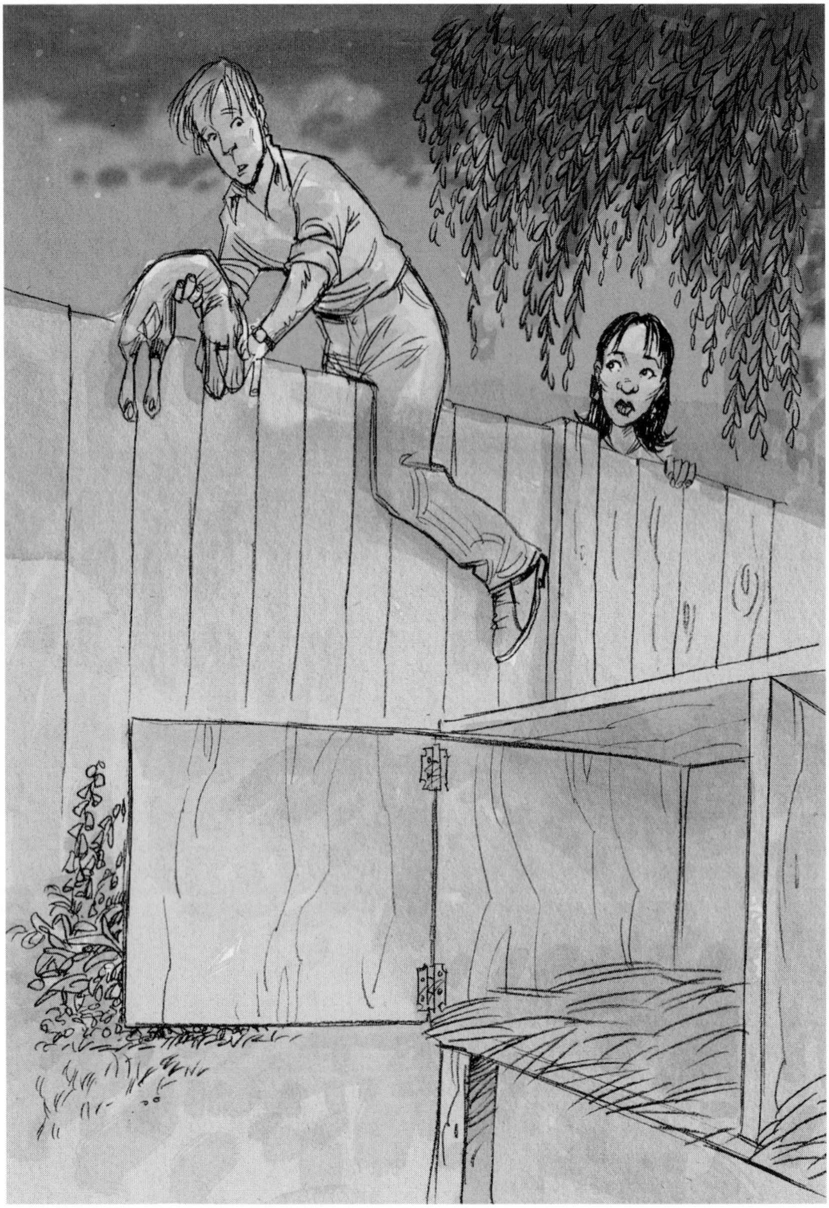

Then the husband had an idea.
'Let's put it back in its hutch,' he said.
'The neighbours will never know what happened.
They'll think it just died naturally!'

'Good idea!' said his wife.
That night, the husband climbed
over the fence.
He put the rabbit back in its hutch.

The next day, the neighbours came back.
The wife saw them in the garden.
'Did you have a nice time?' she asked.

'Yes,' said her neighbour.
'But something a bit strange has happened.
Did you see anyone getting into our garden?'

'No,' said the woman. 'Why?'

'Well,' said the neighbour, 'our rabbit died
just before we went away.
We buried it in the garden,
but now it's back in the hutch!'

6
The Hitch-Hiker

A young woman is driving home late at night.
It's cold, windy and pouring with rain.
She sees an old woman at the side of the road,
trying to hitch a lift.
She takes pity on the old woman
and stops the car.

The old woman gets in.
They chat as they drive along.
The old woman has a very deep voice.
The young woman starts to feel worried.
She notices that the woman has very big hands,
and hairy wrists.

The young woman gets more and more worried.
She is sure that her passenger
is a man dressed up,
so she pretends the car has stalled.

'Do you think you could get out
and give the car a push?'

'All right,' grunts the passenger.
As soon as she – or he – gets out,
the young woman puts her foot on the gas.
She drives away.

A few kilometres down the road,
she sees that the passenger
left a handbag in her car.
She stops.
She opens the bag.

There is nothing inside
except a long, sharp knife.

This is a very old urban myth.
It was first told over 200 years ago.
In those days,
the car was a horse and carriage,
of course.

7
The Kangaroo

This is an Australian urban myth.
It's about a group of young men on holiday
who were driving round the outback
in a camper van.

One day, they hit a kangaroo.
They got out and looked at it.
It was dead, or seemed to be.

One of the lads thought it would be a laugh
to dress the kangaroo up.
He took off his sunglasses
and put them on the kangaroo.
Then he took off his jacket
and put it round the kangaroo's shoulders.

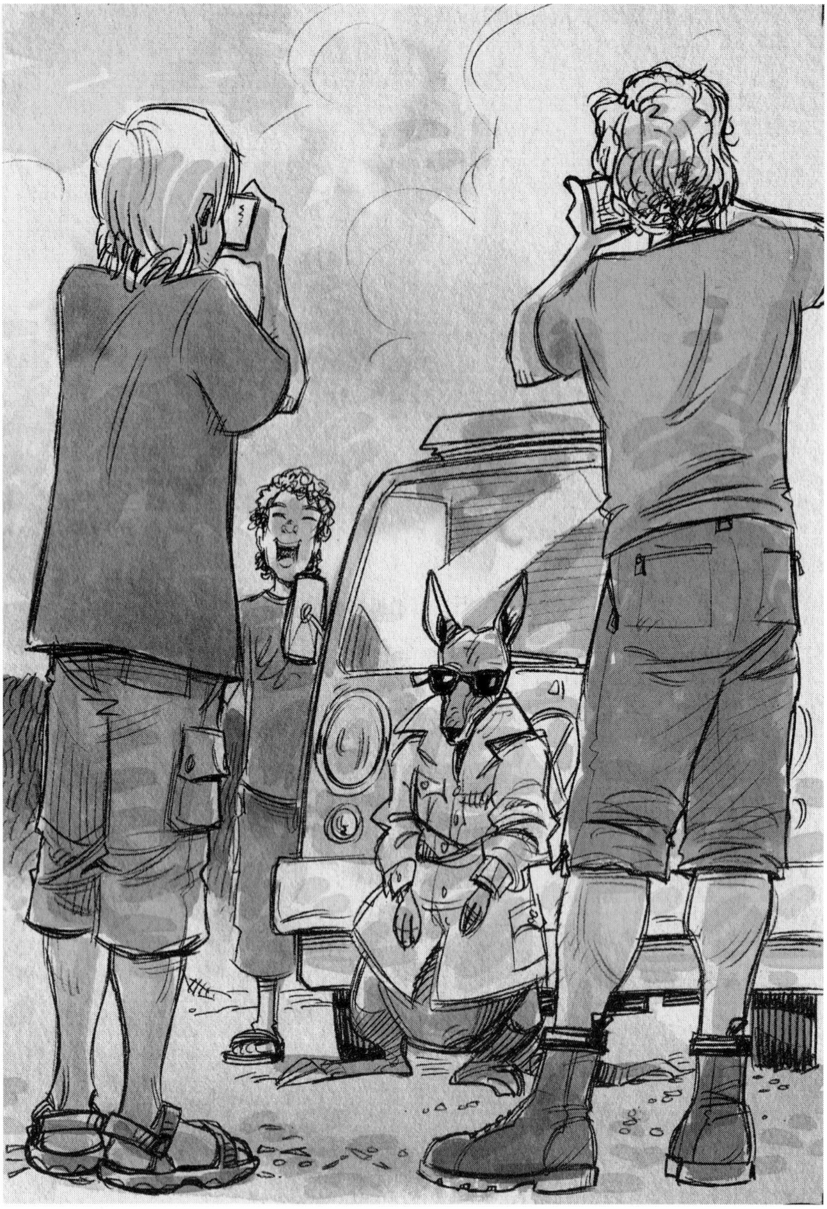

His friends thought this was really funny.
They leaned the kangaroo up against
the front of the van.
They took pictures of it.
They couldn't stop laughing.

Suddenly, the kangaroo came to life.
It wasn't dead, but only stunned.
It went bouncing away across the outback.
Still wearing the jacket and sunglasses.

The young men stopped laughing.
'Quick!' said the man whose jacket it was.
'After it! My credit cards are in that jacket!'

'OK,' said his friends.
'We'll soon catch up with it.
Where are the keys to the van?'

'In my jacket pocket,' he replied …

8
Prawns

A lot of urban myths are about revenge.
This is one of them.

A man and a woman split up
after living together for quite a few years.
The man has found
a younger, more attractive partner.

Before she leaves,
the woman unscrews the brass knobs on the bed.
She drops a pint of prawns
down each of the bed legs.
Then she screws the brass knobs back on.

The man's new partner moves in.
As the weather gets warmer,
the prawns start to rot.
A terrible smell fills the house.
The couple have no idea
where the smell is coming from.
They clean the house from top to bottom,
but the smell just gets worse.

At last they can stand it no longer.
They decide to move.

They find it hard to sell the house.
People are put off by the smell.
In the end they have to sell
the house for about a quarter of its value.
They have to move to a much smaller place.

The day they move out,
the man's ex-partner is watching
from across the road.
She sees the brass bed being loaded
into the removal van, and smiles.

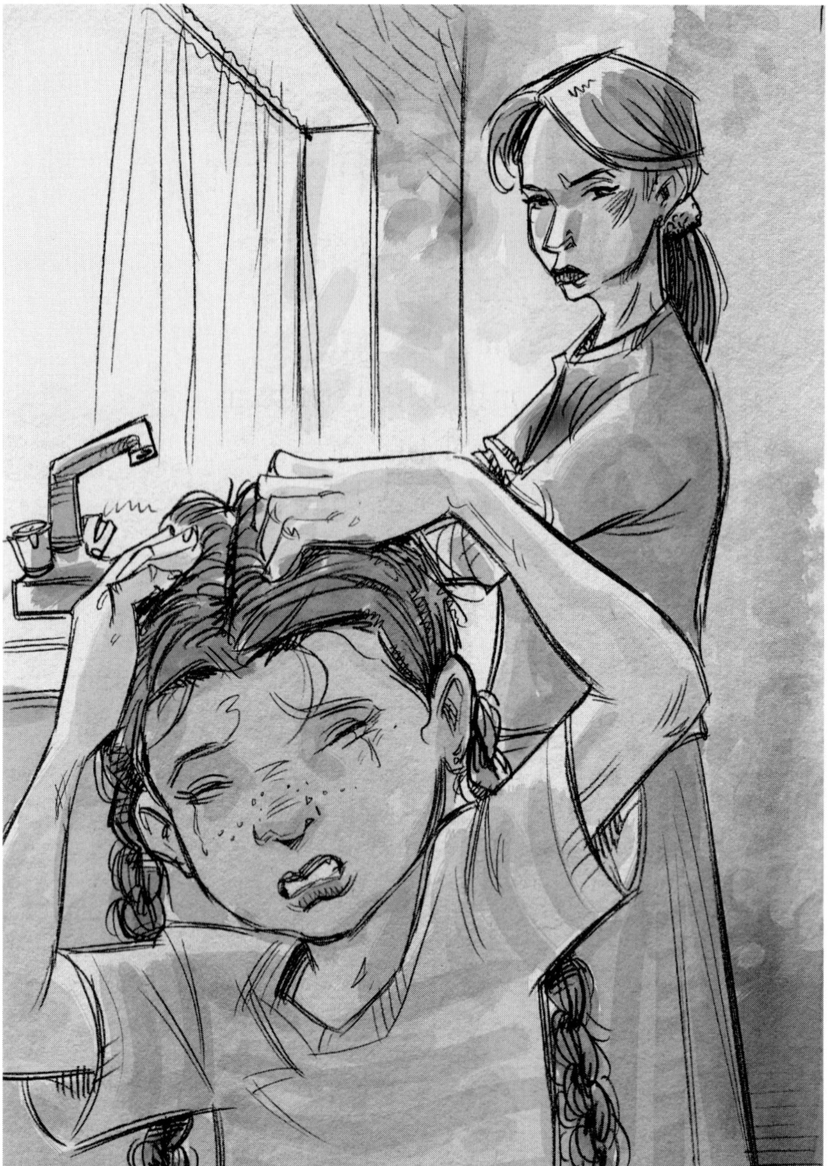

9
Spider in the Hair

A little girl had her hair in plaits.
She never washed or brushed her hair.
Her mum never told her to.
No one had untied them for three months.

The girl began to complain of headaches.
Her mum didn't take any notice.
The mother couldn't be bothered
to take the girl to the doctor.

The pains got worse.
One day, the girl was complaining
about them at school.
Then she fainted.

The teacher untied her hair
to look at her head.
A great big spider crawled out.

The spider had laid eggs in her hair.
The eggs had hatched.
The tiny spiders were eating into her head.
The teacher called an ambulance,
but it was too late.
The girl died in hospital.

This is one of the oldest urban myths.
One version dates back to the Middle Ages.

Stories like this stay popular
because we like strange stories.
We like to think they are true,
that someone we know has a contact
who was involved.
This book gives just a small selection
of urban myths.
There are hundreds more.
Do you know any?